C000303100

RELEASE *your* INNER LIONESS

EMPOWERING QUOTES FROM KICK-ASS WOMEN IN SPORT

summersdale

RELEASE YOUR INNER LIONESS

Compiled by Jess Zahra

An Hachette UK Company
www.hachette.co.uk

Summersdale Publishers Ltd
Part of Octopus Publishing Group Limited
Carmelite House
50 Victoria Embankment
LONDON
EC4Y 0DZ
UK

www.summersdale.com

Printed and bound in China

ISBN: 978-1-80007-918-2

Substantial discounts on bulk quantities of Summersdale books are available to corporations, professional associations and other organizations. For details contact general enquiries: telephone: +44 (0) 1243 771107 or email: enquiries@summersdale.com.

TO

....

FROM

....

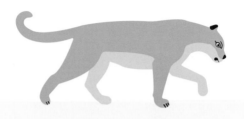

THE MIND IS THE MOST IMPORTANT TOOL. CONQUER THAT, AND YOU CAN ACHIEVE ANYTHING.

BETHANY ENGLAND,
ENGLISH FOOTBALL PLAYER

MY COACH SAID I RUN LIKE A GIRL, AND I SAID IF HE RAN A LITTLE FASTER HE COULD TOO.

MIA HAMM,
AMERICAN FOOTBALL PLAYER

A WOMAN
is unstoppable as soon as

SHE REALIZES

HER POWER

TODAY, DO WHAT
OTHERS WON'T,
SO TOMORROW YOU
CAN ACCOMPLISH
WHAT OTHERS CAN'T.

SIMONE BILES,
AMERICAN GYMNAST

BELIEVE IN YOURSELF WHEN NO ONE ELSE DOES – THAT MAKES YOU A WINNER RIGHT THERE.

VENUS WILLIAMS,
AMERICAN TENNIS PLAYER

FEEL FEARLESS TO SUCCEED.

TORI BOWIE,
AMERICAN TRACK AND
FIELD ATHLETE

YOU WERE NEVER LITTLE RED RIDING HOOD. YOU WERE ALWAYS THE WOLF.

ABBY WAMBACH,
AMERICAN FOOTBALL PLAYER

YOU ONLY LIVE
ONCE AND YOU
NEED TO ENJOY LIFE,
to go out and
achieve whatever
you want to.

ELLIE SIMMONDS,
BRITISH SWIMMER

BELIEVE ME, THE REWARD IS NOT SO GREAT WITHOUT THE STRUGGLE.

WILMA RUDOLPH,
AMERICAN TRACK AND FIELD ATHLETE

SUCCESS BELONGS TO THOSE

WHO WORK HARD ENOUGH FOR IT

I'VE HAD THE FIGHT
IN ME TO TRAIN HARD.
I'LL NEVER BE

out-trained,

THAT'S WHAT I PRIDE
MYSELF ON. I MIGHT NOT
BE THE FASTEST,
THE STRONGEST, BUT

I'll graft

MY ARSE OFF TO GET THERE.

ELLIE ROEBUCK,
ENGLISH FOOTBALL PLAYER

FAILURE I CAN LIVE WITH. NOT TRYING IS WHAT I CAN'T HANDLE!

SANYA RICHARDS-ROSS,
JAMAICAN-AMERICAN
TRACK AND FIELD ATHLETE

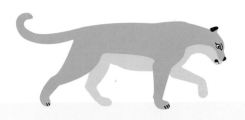

WORK HARD AT BEING THE BEST VERSION OF YOURSELF.

ISADORA DUNCAN,
AMERICAN DANCER

WHEN ANYONE TELLS ME I CAN'T DO ANYTHING, I'M JUST NOT LISTENING ANYMORE.

FLORENCE GRIFFITH JOYNER,
AMERICAN TRACK AND FIELD ATHLETE

THERE'S NOTHING MASCULINE ABOUT BEING COMPETITIVE.

THERE'S NOTHING MASCULINE ABOUT TRYING TO BE THE BEST AT EVERYTHING YOU DO.

REBECCA LOBO, AMERICAN BASKETBALL PLAYER

I DON'T THINK THERE IS ANYTHING WRONG WITH JUST QUIETLY BELIEVING IN YOURSELF.

JESSICA ENNIS-HILL,
BRITISH TRACK AND FIELD ATHLETE

IT'S HARD TO BEAT A WOMAN WHO NEVER GIVES UP

YOU CAN'T ALWAYS BE THE BEST. YOU HAVE TO REMEMBER THAT EVERYONE MAKES MISTAKES SOMETIMES.

ALY RAISMAN,
AMERICAN GYMNAST

IT IS IMPORTANT
TO HAVE A TEST AND...
PROVE TO YOURSELF
THAT YOU CAN
COME THROUGH
THE OTHER SIDE.

LEAH WILLIAMSON,
ENGLISH FOOTBALL PLAYER

WITHOUT YOUR
DOWNS, WITHOUT
YOUR HARDSHIPS,
*I don't think you
appreciate the
ups as much.*

MICHELLE WIE WEST,
AMERICAN GOLFER

THE GREATEST ASSET IS A STRONG MIND.

P. V. SINDHU,
INDIAN BADMINTON PLAYER

I'M LIKE A

comeback kid

– YOU CAN'T

keep me down

FOR LONG!

NICOLA ADAMS,
BRITISH BOXER

WHAT YOU BUILD
IN THE DARK WILL BE
WHAT SUPPORTS YOU WHEN
IT IS TIME TO SHINE.

KELLY CLARK,
AMERICAN SNOWBOARDER

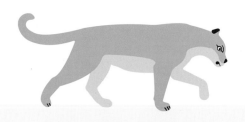

NEVER SET LIMITS, GO AFTER YOUR DREAMS, DON'T BE AFRAID TO PUSH THE BOUNDARIES. AND LAUGH A LOT – IT'S GOOD FOR YOU!

PAULA RADCLIFFE,
BRITISH LONG-DISTANCE RUNNER

BE BOLD.
IF YOU'RE
GOING TO MAKE
AN ERROR,
MAKE A DOOZY,
AND DON'T BE
AFRAID TO HIT
THE BALL.

BILLIE JEAN KING,
AMERICAN TENNIS PLAYER

I WAS 12
WHEN I STARTED
AND 34 BEFORE I
ACHIEVED MY DREAM.
**THAT SHOULD GIVE
PEOPLE HOPE.**

KELLY HOLMES,
BRITISH MIDDLE-DISTANCE RUNNER

EVEN THE SEEMINGLY SMALL THINGS MATTER IF YOU WANT TO BE SUCCESSFUL.

JORDANNE WHILEY,
BRITISH TENNIS PLAYER

I TOTALLY EXPECT THERE
TO BE A YOUNG BOY OR
GIRL SEEING ME AND
GOING ON TO BE BETTER
THAN ME, AND THAT'S
WHAT I WANT TO SEE.

KADEENA COX,
BRITISH CYCLIST AND
TRACK AND FIELD ATHLETE

I DON'T RUN AWAY
FROM A CHALLENGE
BECAUSE I AM AFRAID.
INSTEAD, I RUN TOWARD
IT BECAUSE THE ONLY
WAY TO ESCAPE FEAR
IS TO TRAMPLE IT
BENEATH YOUR FEET.

NADIA COMĂNECI,
ROMANIAN GYMNAST

BEHIND EVERY SUCCESSFUL WOMAN

IS HER TRIBE OF SUPPORTIVE SISTERS

WE WILL PUSH

EACH OTHER

to new levels.

MILLIE BRIGHT,
ENGLISH FOOTBALL PLAYER

I THINK THAT WHEN WE STAND IN SOLIDARITY, WE'LL BE STRONGER.

IBTIHAJ MUHAMMAD,
AMERICAN FENCER

EVERY WOMAN'S

success

SHOULD BE AN

inspiration

TO ANOTHER.

SERENA WILLIAMS,
AMERICAN TENNIS PLAYER

IF YOU CARE
ABOUT THE PEOPLE
YOU WORK WITH, THEN
YOU WORK HARDER.

KRISTINE LILLY,
AMERICAN FOOTBALL PLAYER

I ALWAYS WANT TO GIVE MORE THAN I GAVE YESTERDAY.

ALLYSON FELIX,
AMERICAN TRACK AND FIELD ATHLETE

I WANT THE YOUNGER
GENERATION OF
GIRLS TO KNOW THAT
ANYTHING IS POSSIBLE,
AND IF YOU PUT
YOUR MIND TO IT,
YOU CAN ACCOMPLISH
IT. WE ARE IN
THIS TOGETHER!

JADA WILLIAMS,
AMERICAN BASKETBALL PLAYER

DO
WHAT
YOU
LOVE

I FEEL MOST AT EASE
WHEN I AM ON THE
PITCH AND PLAYING
WITH A SMILE.

GEORGIA STANWAY,
ENGLISH FOOTBALL PLAYER

I DON'T RACE BECAUSE I LOVE WINNING. I RACE BECAUSE I LOVE RACING.

MADISON DE ROZARIO,
AUSTRALIAN WHEELCHAIR RACER

BEING NERVOUS IS NOT SOMETHING YOU SHOULD BE ASHAMED OF. NERVOUS MEANS YOU CARE, YOU REALLY WANT TO DO WELL.

PAULA CREAMER,
AMERICAN GOLFER

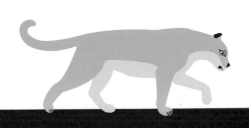

A TROPHY CARRIES DUST. MEMORIES LAST FOREVER.

MARY LOU RETTON,
AMERICAN GYMNAST

IN LIFE, JUST FIND SOMETHING YOU LOVE AND MAKE IT YOUR LIFE. THAT IS THE ONLY WAY TO BE SUCCESSFUL. *Love what you do.*

HANNAH COCKROFT,
BRITISH WHEELCHAIR RACER

YES, I'M A GIRLY GIRL AND YES, I LOVE SPORT. TIME TO SHOW US GIRLS CAN DO BOTH.

AMBER HILL,
BRITISH SPORT SHOOTER

NEVER

apologize

FOR YOUR

POWER

IT GOT TO A POINT WHERE *a teacher* WAS LIKE, "JUST LET HER PLAY WITH THE BOYS. *She's not bringing the level down,* SHE'S BRINGING IT UP!"

RACHEL DALY,
ENGLISH FOOTBALL PLAYER

A PERSON'S
VIEW OF YOU IS
NOT IMPORTANT. WHAT
IS IMPORTANT IS YOUR
VIEW OF YOURSELF.

**SHELLY-ANN FRASER-PRYCE,
JAMAICAN TRACK AND
FIELD ATHLETE**

SOME PEOPLE LIKE TO CALL ME COCKY OR ARROGANT, BUT I JUST THINK, "HOW DARE YOU ASSUME I SHOULD THINK LESS OF MYSELF?"

RONDA ROUSEY,
AMERICAN WRESTLER AND
MIXED MARTIAL ARTIST

DON'T LET ANYONE TELL YOU YOU'RE WEAK BECAUSE YOU ARE A WOMAN.

MARY KOM,
INDIAN BOXER

YOU HAVE THE POWER
TO BE ANYTHING YOU
WANT TO BE.

TATYANA MCFADDEN,
AMERICAN WHEELCHAIR RACER

IF THE STABLE GATE IS CLOSED, CLIMB THE FENCE.

JULIE KRONE,
AMERICAN JOCKEY

A CHANCE NOT TAKEN IS AN OPPORTUNITY MISSED

WHEN THINGS DON'T GO
RIGHT FOR ME IN THE
WAY THAT I HOPED THEY
WOULD, I WANT TO PROVE
PEOPLE WRONG AND IT
MOTIVATES ME MORE.

BETH MEAD,
ENGLISH FOOTBALL PLAYER

YOU PROBABLY LEARN MORE FROM BAD EXPERIENCES THAN YOU DO THE GOOD ONES.

REBECCA ADLINGTON,
BRITISH SWIMMER

IT'S NOT ABOUT
THE ACTUAL
FAILURE ITSELF;
it's how you
respond to it.

ABBY WAMBACH,
AMERICAN FOOTBALL PLAYER

EVERY MORNING I AM A BEGINNER.

HANYA HOLM,
AMERICAN DANCER

WHEN YOU FALL,
GET RIGHT BACK UP.

Just keep going,

KEEP PUSHING IT.

LINDSEY VONN,
AMERICAN ALPINE SKI RACER

THE KEY IS THAT
I CONTROL MY LIFE;
MY LIFE DOESN'T
CONTROL ME.

GABRIELLE REECE,
AMERICAN VOLLEYBALL PLAYER

KEEP
YOUR

HEAD
UP

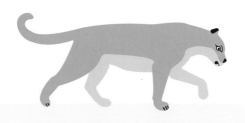

HAVE FAITH IN YOURSELF AND GO TAKE THAT FIRST STEP. IF I COULD, SO CAN YOU.

HEENA SIDHU,
INDIAN SPORT SHOOTER

I'D RATHER REGRET THE RISKS THAT DIDN'T WORK OUT THAN THE CHANCES I DIDN'T TAKE AT ALL.

SIMONE BILES,
AMERICAN GYMNAST

JUST SEIZE
EVERY OPPORTUNITY
YOU HAVE, EMBRACE
EVERY EXPERIENCE.
MAKE A MARK,
FOR ALL THE
RIGHT REASONS.

CHRISSIE WELLINGTON,
BRITISH TRIATHLETE

IF YOU WANT TO ACHIEVE SOMETHING IN LIFE, YOU HAVE TO TAKE RISKS.

DIPA KARMAKAR,
INDIAN GYMNAST

I WANT TO LAY ALL
MY CARDS OUT
ON THE TABLE AND
WALK AWAY WITH
NO REGRETS.

KATARINA JOHNSON-THOMPSON,
BRITISH HEPTATHLETE

TAKE THOSE CHANCES
AND YOU CAN ACHIEVE
GREATNESS, WHEREAS IF
YOU GO CONSERVATIVE,
YOU'LL NEVER KNOW...
Even if you fail,
learning and moving
on is sometimes
the best thing.

DANICA PATRICK,
AMERICAN RACE CAR DRIVER

I'M ADDICTED TO WINNING, AND IT'S SOMETHING I CAME HERE TO DO.

ALEX GREENWOOD,
ENGLISH FOOTBALL PLAYER

YOU SHOULD NEVER STAY AT THE SAME LEVEL. ALWAYS PUSH YOURSELF TO THE NEXT.

MARNELLI DIMZON,
PHILIPPINE FOOTBALL PLAYER

I ALWAYS BELIEVE I
CAN BEAT THE BEST,

achieve the best.

I ALWAYS SEE MYSELF IN

the top position.

SERENA WILLIAMS,
AMERICAN TENNIS PLAYER

THE IMPORTANT
THING IS NOT TO
RETREAT; YOU HAVE TO
MASTER YOURSELF.

OLGA KORBUT,
BELARUSIAN GYMNAST

THAT WALL IS YOUR MIND PLAYING TRICKS ON YOU. YOU JUST NEED TO SAY, "ONE MORE STEP, I CAN DO THIS. I HAVE MORE IN ME."

KERRI WALSH JENNINGS,
AMERICAN BEACH VOLLEYBALL PLAYER

YOU'LL NEVER KNOW WHAT YOU'RE CAPABLE OF UNTIL YOU TAKE THAT FIRST STEP AND JUST GO FOR IT.

NATASHA HASTINGS,
AMERICAN TRACK AND FIELD SPRINTER

THERE IS A TIME TO PUSH YOURSELF,

AND THERE IS A TIME TO REST

WHEREVER I AM,
I'M PRESENT,
AND HOPEFULLY
THINGS FALL
INTO PLACE.

MARY EARPS,
ENGLISH FOOTBALL PLAYER

EVERYTHING IS GOING TO WORK OUT – THERE'S NO OTHER OPTION.

KARI MILLER,
AMERICAN VOLLEYBALL PLAYER

OUR BEST DAYS
ARE AHEAD OF US.
STAY POSITIVELY
OPTIMISTIC AND
WORK YOUR BUTT OFF.

ALIPHINE TULIAMUK,
AMERICAN LONG-DISTANCE RUNNER

I DON'T KNOW THE SECRET TO SUCCESS, BUT I'M PRETTY SURE THE CLOSEST THING IS PREPARATION.

MICHELLE KWAN,
AMERICAN FIGURE SKATER

I BREAK, BUT I GET
BACK UP AGAIN,
and I keep going.

MCKENZIE COAN,
AMERICAN SWIMMER

WE'RE NEVER ABOVE YOU, NEVER BELOW YOU, BUT BESIDE YOU.

FIAO'O FA'AMAUSILI,
NEW ZEALAND RUGBY PLAYER

**BAD
EXPERIENCES
ARE LESSONS,
NOT FAILURES**

IF WE'RE NOT
making mistakes
THEN, FOR US
as a group,
WE'RE NOT BEING
BRAVE ENOUGH.

MILLIE BRIGHT,
ENGLISH FOOTBALL PLAYER

THE PAST DOESN'T MATTER. TAKE TODAY.

BECKY SAUERBRUNN,
AMERICAN FOOTBALL PLAYER

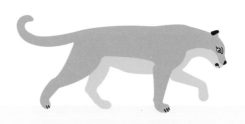

A FAILURE ISN'T A FAILURE IF IT PREPARES YOU FOR SUCCESS TOMORROW.

LOLO JONES,
AMERICAN BOBSLEDDER
AND HURDLER

WE CAN ALL FIND
WAYS TO SUPPORT
THE PEOPLE AROUND
US. WE CAN ALL
FIND A PURPOSE ON
THIS EARTH LARGER
THAN OURSELVES.

DANIELLE GREEN,
AMERICAN BASKETBALL PLAYER

YOU CAN'T LET
YOUR CURRENT
CIRCUMSTANCES
DICTATE WHAT
KIND OF CHOICES
YOU MAKE.

KELLY CLARK,
AMERICAN SNOWBOARDER

DEFEAT DRIVES YOU TO WIN.

ANGELIQUE KERBER,
GERMAN TENNIS PLAYER

YOUR

BEST IS

ENOUGH

BEING THE BEST IS
APPLYING YOURSELF
TO YOUR POTENTIAL,
PUTTING OUT THE BEST
VERSION OF YOURSELF.

NIKITA PARRIS,
ENGLISH FOOTBALL PLAYER

I DO MY BEST, AND THAT'S ALL I CAN DO.

CAROLINE WOZNIACKI,
DANISH TENNIS PLAYER

A SUCCESSFUL COMPETITION FOR ME IS ALWAYS GOING OUT THERE AND PUTTING 100 PER CENT INTO WHATEVER I'M DOING. *It's not always winning.*

SIMONE BILES,
AMERICAN GYMNAST

DON'T LET YOUR FEAR DECIDE YOUR FUTURE.

SHALANE FLANAGAN,
AMERICAN LONG-DISTANCE RUNNER

I TREASURE

the power

AND

beauty

OF MY BODY.

LYNN JENNINGS,
AMERICAN LONG-DISTANCE RUNNER

NEVER LET THE FEAR
OF FAILING DISCOURAGE
YOU FROM TRYING.

SUE BIRD,
AMERICAN BASKETBALL PLAYER

YOU
ARE

IN
CONTROL

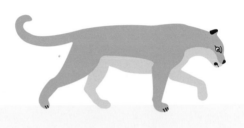

EDUCATE, DON'T RETALIATE.

DEMI STOKES,
ENGLISH FOOTBALL PLAYER

I'M STRONG, I'M TOUGH, I STILL WEAR MY EYELINER.

LISA LESLIE,
AMERICAN BASKETBALL PLAYER

YOU'VE GOT TO TRY TO
DO WHAT YOU WANT
TO DO IN LIFE AND
**NOT LET PEOPLE TELL
YOU WHAT TO DO.**

HANNAH HAMPTON,
ENGLISH FOOTBALL PLAYER

I'M STRONGER
THAN I THINK
I AM.

MISTY MAY-TREANOR,
AMERICAN BEACH VOLLEYBALL PLAYER

I PUSH MYSELF TO BE
THE BEST I CAN BE. I
DON'T WORRY ABOUT
WHAT OTHER PEOPLE ARE
DOING, AND I DON'T
THINK ABOUT THINGS
I CAN'T CONTROL.

ANNIKA SÖRENSTAM,
SWEDISH GOLFER

YOU CAN ACHIEVE SO MANY AMAZING GOALS AND GET SUCH AMAZING OPPORTUNITIES IF YOU WORK HARD AND APPLY YOURSELF TO THINGS.

DINA ASHER-SMITH,
BRITISH SPRINTER

YOU ARE
THE ONLY
ONE THAT CAN
LIMIT YOUR
GREATNESS

WHEN YOU'RE HAPPY
IN A PLACE AND AN
ENVIRONMENT WITH
THE PEOPLE THAT
ARE AROUND YOU,
the sky is the limit.

LOTTE WUBBEN-MOY,
ENGLISH FOOTBALL PLAYER

I KNOW WITH THE LOWS WILL BE HIGHS. I JUST HAVE TO MAKE THEM HAPPEN.

ELLIE ROEBUCK,
ENGLISH FOOTBALL PLAYER

I AM NOT LOOKING TO ESCAPE THE PRESSURE.

I am embracing it.

PRESSURE IS WHAT BUILDS UP IN THE CHAMBER BEHIND THE BULLET BEFORE

it explodes out of the gun.

RONDA ROUSEY,
AMERICAN WRESTLER AND
MIXED MARTIAL ARTIST

I BELIEVE IN THE IMPOSSIBLE BECAUSE NO ONE ELSE DOES.

FLORENCE GRIFFITH JOYNER,
AMERICAN TRACK AND
FIELD ATHLETE

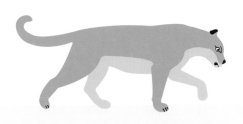

IT'S ALL ABOUT NOT DOING WHAT EVERYONE ELSE IS DOING BUT TO MAKE YOUR OWN PRESENCE COUNT.

ANJUM CHOPRA,
INDIAN CRICKETER

A CHAMPION IS DEFINED NOT BY THEIR WINS BUT BY HOW THEY CAN RECOVER WHEN THEY FALL.

SERENA WILLIAMS,
AMERICAN TENNIS PLAYER

DON'T *run away from* **CHALLENGES. RUN OVER THEM.**

THE ONLY ONE
WHO CAN TELL YOU,
"YOU CAN'T WIN,"
IS YOU,
AND YOU DON'T
HAVE TO LISTEN.

JESSICA ENNIS-HILL,
BRITISH TRACK AND FIELD ATHLETE

LIFE'S A CHALLENGE, BUT THAT'S THE BEST PART.

VENUS WILLIAMS,
AMERICAN TENNIS PLAYER

I AM BUILDING A
FIRE, AND EVERY DAY
I TRAIN, I ADD MORE
FUEL. AT JUST THE
RIGHT MOMENT,
I LIGHT THE MATCH.

MIA HAMM,
AMERICAN FOOTBALL PLAYER

WHAT THREATENS
TO WEAKEN YOU
WILL NOT OVERCOME
YOU. YOU WILL
CONQUER. YOU
ARE IN CONTROL.

ELLIE ROBINSON,
BRITISH SWIMMER

HARD DAYS ARE
THE BEST BECAUSE
that's when
champions
are made.

GABBY DOUGLAS,
AMERICAN GYMNAST

THERE'S NO LIMIT TO WHAT I CAN DO.

LEYLAH FERNANDEZ,
CANADIAN TENNIS PLAYER

YOU

DO
YOU

I WOULDN'T HAVE
changed
THE PATH I TOOK...
The experiences
THAT I HAVE GOT,
THEY ARE PRICELESS.

LUCY BRONZE,
ENGLISH FOOTBALL PLAYER

PEOPLE WOULD SAY,
"GIRLS DON'T PLAY HOCKEY.
GIRLS DON'T SKATE." I
WOULD SAY, "WATCH THIS."

HAYLEY WICKENHEISER,
CANADIAN ICE HOCKEY PLAYER

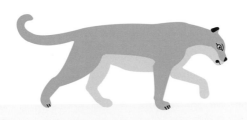

I WAS NOT BORN TO BE A CHAMPION. I FOUGHT TO BE A CHAMPION.

BECKY LYNCH,
IRISH WRESTLER

I WANT TO TELL
GIRLS, IT'S NOT
ABOUT MAKE-UP
AND HOW YOU LOOK
THAT'S IMPORTANT:
YOU ARE SO MUCH
MORE THAN HOW
YOU LOOK.

KATIE TAYLOR,
IRISH BOXER

WE HAVE
THE POWER
TO CHOOSE
OUR STORY.

MELISSA STOCKWELL,
AMERICAN SWIMMER
AND TRIATHLETE

IF YOU MESS UP,
DON'T PANIC.
THERE'S ALWAYS
A SOLUTION TO
THE PROBLEM,
AND LEARNING
FROM YOUR
MISTAKES IS
ONE OF THE
MOST IMPORTANT
LESSONS IN LIFE.

BETH TWEDDLE,
BRITISH GYMNAST

YOU ARE STRONG ENOUGH TO SOLVE EVEN THE TOUGHEST PROBLEMS

ANY GIRL CAN DO
WHAT I DID; ALL THEY
NEED IS DOGGEDNESS,
DETERMINATION, THE WILL
TO PUSH HARD AND PUSH
THROUGH BOUNDARIES, AND
NEVER-ENDING COMMITMENT
TO ACHIEVE THEIR GOAL.

SAKSHI MALIK,
INDIAN WRESTLER

ALWAYS WORK HARD, NEVER GIVE UP, AND FIGHT UNTIL THE END BECAUSE IT'S NEVER REALLY OVER UNTIL THE WHISTLE BLOWS.

ALEX MORGAN,
AMERICAN FOOTBALL PLAYER

WE ARE
HUMAN BEINGS,
AT THE END
OF THE DAY.
Success and
failure are a
part and parcel
of our life.

HIMA DAS,
INDIAN SPRINTER

MY PHILOSOPHY IS NOT TO BE SCARED OF ANYONE.

SAINA NEHWAL,
INDIAN BADMINTON PLAYER

YOU NEVER KNOW IF
YOU CAN ACTUALLY
DO SOMETHING

against all odds

UNTIL YOU

actually do it.

ABBY WAMBACH,
AMERICAN FOOTBALL PLAYER

I WANT TO DO
SOMETHING SPECIAL,
THAT IS HISTORIC AND
UNFORGETTABLE.

TIRUNESH DIBABA,
ETHIOPIAN
LONG-DISTANCE RUNNER

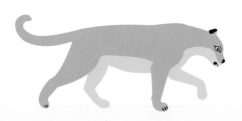

IF I, BEING A
MOTHER OF TWO,
CAN WIN A MEDAL,
SO CAN YOU ALL.
TAKE ME AS AN
EXAMPLE AND
DON'T GIVE UP.

MARY KOM,
INDIAN BOXER

I ALWAYS TRY TO START OUT WITH SOME TYPE OF GOAL. THEN I WORK BACKWARD AND THINK OF WHAT I NEED TO DO TO GET THERE, AND GIVE MYSELF SMALLER GOALS THAT ARE MORE IMMEDIATE.

KRISTI YAMAGUCHI,
AMERICAN FIGURE SKATER

ALL YOU NEED IS THE
COURAGE TO BELIEVE
IN YOURSELF AND
PUT ONE FOOT IN
FRONT OF THE OTHER.

KATHRINE SWITZER,
AMERICAN MARATHON RUNNER

I'D RATHER BE INSPIRED BY MY COMPETITION THAN BE JEALOUS.

JAMIE ANDERSON,
AMERICAN SNOWBOARDER

THE ONLY PERSON WHO CAN STOP YOU FROM REACHING YOUR GOALS IS YOU.

JACKIE JOYNER-KERSEE,
AMERICAN TRACK AND FIELD ATHLETE

I JUST KNEW IF IT COULD BE DONE, IT HAD TO BE DONE, AND I DID IT.

GERTRUDE EDERLE,
AMERICAN SWIMMER

NOTHING
WORTH
HAVING

COMES
EASILY

Putting yourself out there is hard, but it's so worth it.

I DON'T THINK ANYONE WHO HAS EVER SPOKEN OUT, OR STOOD UP OR HAD A BRAVE MOMENT, HAS REGRETTED IT.

MEGAN RAPINOE,
AMERICAN FOOTBALL PLAYER

WE HAVE THE POWER TO CREATE CHANGE AND INSPIRE PEOPLE.

SASHA DIGIULIAN,
AMERICAN ROCK CLIMBER

AS LONG AS YOU ARE

prepared,

WORK HARD AND

know your stuff,

YOU WILL BE FINE.

MEGAN ALEXANDER,
ENGLISH FOOTBALL PLAYER

IT ONLY TAKES
ONE PERSON TO
CREATE A MOVEMENT.

ASMA ELBADAWI,
SUDANESE-BRITISH
BASKETBALL PLAYER

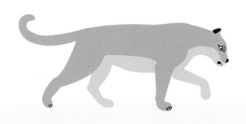

I DON'T FOCUS
ON WHAT I'M UP
AGAINST. I FOCUS ON
MY GOALS AND I TRY
TO IGNORE THE REST.

VENUS WILLIAMS,
AMERICAN TENNIS PLAYER

IF YOU PERSEVERE LONG ENOUGH, IF YOU DO THE RIGHT THINGS LONG ENOUGH, THE RIGHT THINGS WILL HAPPEN.

MANON RHÉAUME,
CANADIAN ICE HOCKEY PLAYER

TURN
YOUR
DREAMS
INTO
PLANS

I NEVER REALLY
SEE MYSELF AS A ROLE
MODEL. I JUST SEE
MYSELF AS BEING ME
AND JUST TRYING TO BE
THE BEST VERSION OF
MYSELF THAT I CAN BE.

JESS CARTER,
ENGLISH FOOTBALL PLAYER

IF YOUR DREAM SOUNDS IMPOSSIBLE: **PERFECT.** YOU'RE ON THE RIGHT TRACK.

JESSICA LONG,
AMERICAN SWIMMER

THERE'S NO SUBSTITUTE
FOR HARD WORK.
IF YOU WORK HARD
AND PREPARE YOURSELF,
YOU MIGHT GET BEAT,
BUT YOU'LL NEVER LOSE.

NANCY LIEBERMAN,
AMERICAN BASKETBALL PLAYER

ERASE THE WORD
"FAILURE" FROM YOUR
VOCABULARY. NO CASE
IS EVER TRULY CLOSED,
AND NO CHALLENGE
IS EVER OVER.

MARY LOU RETTON,
AMERICAN GYMNAST

WOMEN: WHEN WE TEAM UP, WE ARE INCREDIBLY POWERFUL. FIND SOMEONE TO TEAM UP WITH...

Our voices collectively really do make a difference, and change and perspective is worth fighting for.

DONNA ORENDER,
AMERICAN BASKETBALL PLAYER

I THINK IN LIFE YOU SHOULD WORK ON YOURSELF UNTIL THE DAY YOU DIE.

SERENA WILLIAMS,
AMERICAN TENNIS PLAYER

PEOPLE WILL

put restrictions

**ON YOUR ABILITY, ON YOUR
APTITUDE, ON YOUR TALENT,
ON YOUR CHARACTER,
AND TO BE HONEST,**

it's just opinion.

**DON'T LET ANYONE PUT
YOU IN A BOX OR DRAW
YOUR PATH FOR YOU.**

VICTORIA PENDLETON,
BRITISH TRACK CYCLIST

CHAMPIONS KEEP PLAYING UNTIL THEY GET IT RIGHT.

BILLIE JEAN KING,
AMERICAN TENNIS PLAYER

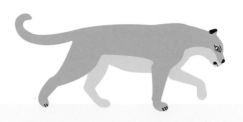

THE POTENTIAL FOR GREATNESS LIVES WITHIN EACH OF US.

WILMA RUDOLPH,
AMERICAN TRACK AND
FIELD ATHLETE

I'M SCARED OF FAILURE ALL THE TIME, BUT I'M NOT SCARED ENOUGH TO STOP TRYING.

RONDA ROUSEY,
AMERICAN WRESTLER AND
MIXED MARTIAL ARTIST

I'M NOT THE NEXT USAIN BOLT OR MICHAEL PHELPS. I'M THE FIRST SIMONE BILES.

SIMONE BILES,
AMERICAN GYMNAST

COURAGE, SACRIFICE, DETERMINATION, COMMITMENT, TOUGHNESS, HEART, TALENT, GUTS. THAT'S WHAT LITTLE GIRLS ARE MADE OF; THE HECK WITH SUGAR AND SPICE.

BETHANY HAMILTON,
AMERICAN SURFER

Have you enjoyed this book? If so, find us
on Facebook at Summersdale Publishers,
on Twitter at @Summersdale and on
Instagram at @summersdalebooks and
get in touch. We'd love to hear from you!

www.summersdale.com